Jesus—the Life Changer

Student Journal

by Kelli and David Trujillo

Group

Loveland, Colorado

Jesus—the Life Changer

•••• Student Journal

Visit our Web site: **www.group.com**

Credits
Editor: Paul Woods
Creative Development Editor: Kate S. Holburn
Chief Creative Officer: Joani Schultz
Copy Editor: Ann Jahns
Art Director: Toolbox Creative
Designer/Illustrator: Toolbox Creative
Cover Art Director: Jeff Storm
Cover Designer: Susan Tripp
Production Manager: Dodie Tipton

ISBN 0-7644-2932-9
10 9 8 7 6 5 4 3 2 1   14 13 12 11 10 09 08 07 06 05

Printed in the United States of America.

Introduction

[Jesus] asked his disciples, "Who do people say the Son of Man is?"
They replied, "Some say John the Baptist; others say Elijah; and still
others, Jeremiah or one of the prophets."
"But what about you?" he asked. "Who do you say I am?"
Simon Peter answered, "You are the Christ, the Son of the living God"
(Matthew 16:13-16).

Jesus. He's the prophesied Messiah, the Word made flesh, the Son of God, the powerful miracle-worker, the Christ, the Anointed One, the Grace-giver, the crucified Lamb, the Resurrection and the Life, the Lion of the tribe of Judah, the Servant, the King…the Life Changer. Over the next 12 weeks, take off on the adventure of knowing him better—your life will be transformed as a result.

The Promised Messiah—Servant or King?

Like any good sleuth, a careful reader of the book of Isaiah quickly discovers that the prophet is leaving us clues—clues about the identity of the coming Messiah. This Messiah would be both a servant and a king. Many other details about the coming Messiah can be found in the Old Testament—he'd be from the line of David (2 Samuel 7:12-13), he'd be born in Bethlehem (Micah 5:2), his mother would be a virgin (Isaiah 7:14), and he'd suffer and die for the sins of the world (Isaiah 53:7-8). Only one man in history fit this profile, and he fit it to a T.

His name is Jesus.

> "Who is he? What sort of hero approaches? What is this Mercy soon to
> be born among us? Why, he shall be a king!…This King shall gather
> time and space into his kingdom, and shall himself embrace the history
> of humankind, for of his kingdom 'there will be no end.' "
> —Walter Wangerin Jr., ***Preparing for Jesus***

ON YOUR OWN

Use these ideas as part of your personal devotional time this week.

• •

Study Isaiah 52:13–53:12 again. How is the coming Messiah described? How is God's love described? What does this description tell us about God's character? What do these verses mean to you personally?

• •

Journal your thoughts about the following: Isaiah 7:14 describes the coming Messiah as *Immanuel,* meaning "God with us." What's significant about this name? What does it say about who God is? What does it say about how God relates to you?

• •

Read the quote from Walter Wangerin Jr., and respond by writing your thoughts.

NOTES, THOUGHTS, AND PRAYERS...

Leading Suspects: Maher-Shalal-Hash-Baz and King Hezekiah

Discuss these questions, and write your answers in the space provided.

Read Isaiah 7:13-17. What clues from this passage might help us identify the Messiah, the hero, in Isaiah? Hint: Look for key phrases and words.

....

....

....

....

Now read about Maher-Shalal-Hash-Baz in Isaiah 8:1-10. What evidence leads us to believe that he is the hero described in 7:13-17? Hint: Look for words and ideas shared between these two verses.

....

....

....

....

Read Isaiah 9:6-7. What additional clues are revealed here about the hero?

....

....

....

....

What is the evidence *against* Maher-Shalal-Hash-Baz as the Messiah, in light of the additional clues of 9:6-7?

....

....

....

....

Now read about King Hezekiah in Isaiah 36:1; 37:30-35; and 38:1-7. Looking back to the clues of 7:13-17 and 9:67, what is the evidence for King Hezekiah as the one who was prophesied?

....

....

....

Read these portions of the following "Servant Songs" from Isaiah: 42:1-4; 49:5-7; 50:4-10; 52:13–53:12. What is the new evidence concerning the Messiah in these passages? How might this be considered a twist in the story?

....

....

....

....

....

Taking into account the third set of clues about the "servant," what evidence now leads us away from King Hezekiah as the "leading suspect," the promised Messiah?

....

....

....

....

....

What sort of Messiah does that leave?

....

....

....

....

....

....

The Birth—O Holy Night!

Christmas trees, stockings hanging over the fireplace, Nativity scenes—these are some of the symbols of the modern celebration of Jesus' birth. It's a great thing to commemorate Jesus' birth once a year, but Christians shouldn't relegate this event to the dusty corners of their mind, dusting it off only when December rolls around. Instead, considering Jesus' birth and the circumstances that surround it should be a regular part of our devotional life. It is through a careful study of Jesus' arrival on this planet that we can discover amazing and fundamental truths about who Jesus is and what his purpose was on earth.

> "What one of us can understand a love so great that we would willingly limit our unlimitedness, put the flesh of mortality over our immortality, accept all the pain and grief of humanity, submit to betrayal by that humanity, be killed by it, and die a total failure (in human terms)…?"
> —Madeleine L'Engle, *The Irrational Season*

ON YOUR OWN

Use these ideas as part of your personal devotional time this week.

• •

Read about Simeon and Anna in Luke 2:21-38. Consider these questions and journal your responses: How did Simeon's and Anna's words shed light on Jesus' purpose? What would you have thought if you were in the temple that day and observed this occurrence? How did Simeon and Anna know that Jesus was the One? How might Simeon's and Anna's words have affected Mary and Joseph?

• •

Reread the words of "O Holy Night" (p. 15), then write a hymn or song of your own describing Jesus' birth.

• •

Read the quote from Madeleine L'Engle, and journal about your personal response to it.

NOTES, THOUGHTS, AND PRAYERS...

_____

_____

_____

_____

_____

_____

_____

_____

_____

_____

_____

_____

_____

Defining *Incarnation*

The word *incarnation* comes from the Latin words *in carne,* which literally mean "in flesh." God, the creator of the universe—the powerful, eternal, loving, ultimate Being—took on human flesh. Because of his love for humanity, he came to earth in the person of Jesus. As the *New Bible Dictionary* explains, "God, without ceasing to be God, was made man... When the Word 'became flesh' his deity was not abandoned, or reduced, or contracted." In other words, Jesus, in a mysterious and divine way that is difficult to comprehend, was both fully God and fully human. He was God...with skin on.

· · · · · · · ·

"The Word became flesh and blood,

and moved into the neighborhood.

We saw the glory with our own eyes,

the one-of-a-kind glory,

like Father, like Son,

Generous inside and out,

true from start to finish."

John 1:14, *The Message*

· · · · · · · ·

Study and Worship Station A— the Pregnancy

Read Matthew 1:18-24 and Luke 1:26-38 with your partner.

Pick up a grain of rice and hold it in your hand. This grain is the approximate size of a 30-day-old human fetus—¼ inch long.

Just 24 days after conception, an embryo's heart begins to beat.

A 6-week-old embryo has arms and legs; toes and fingers are starting to develop. Brain waves can be detected.

A 9-week-old embryo has all the important organs. The liver and kidneys begin to work. Fingerprints, taste buds, and fingernails have begun to form.

By about six months, when the baby is about 10 inches long, he or she can hear sounds.

During the last few months of pregnancy, a baby can recognize the parents' voices, develops sleeping patterns, practices "breathing" amniotic fluid, opens and closes his or her eyes, responds to pain and light, and can suck a thumb for comfort.

Discuss these questions with your partner:

- **What thoughts or feelings come to mind when you consider that God, the creator of the universe, went through all these stages of human development? What amazes you the most?**

- **How do these details about human development—and considering that God went through each of these stages—impact or alter your understanding of the incarnation?**

Take a few minutes to write down a few notes from this station on page 14. What stood out to you the most? Why? Be sure to write your answer to this question:

- **What do we learn about Jesus—his traits and his purpose— from these Scripture passages?**

When you're done taking notes, move to the next station with your partner.

Study and Worship Station B— the Birth

Turn to your partner and describe a hospital room. What is it like? What comforts, safety measures, or medical technologies are provided? How would these measures help a pregnant woman to experience a safe delivery of her baby?

Use the hand sanitizer gel (or wipes) at the station to sanitize your hands.

Now read Luke 2:1-7.

Jesus wasn't born in a comfortable, sterile, peaceful hospital room. Mary labored and delivered Jesus in a place that was likely a stable or cave. She wasn't attended to by doctors and nurses—her "delivery room staff" probably included donkeys, sheep, or other animals. It was dirty and probably smelled of straw, dirty animals, and perhaps even manure. It was not peaceful. It was not comfortable. And it was definitely not sanitized.

Discuss these questions with your partner:

- **Since God is all-powerful, why didn't he arrange things so Jesus could have been born in a different setting—like in a palace or at least in a home?**

- **Is this the type of birth most people at that time probably expected for the coming Messiah? Explain.**

- **What are five adjectives you could use to describe the setting and circumstances of Jesus' birth?**

- **What does the setting of Jesus' birth indicate about Jesus—his traits and his purpose?**

Take a few minutes to write down a few notes from this station on page 14. What stood out to you the most? Why? And be sure to write your answer to this question:

- **What do we learn about Jesus—his traits and his purpose—from this Scripture passage?**

When you're done taking notes, move to the next station with your partner.

Study and Worship Station C— Jesus' Visitors

Read about those who visited Jesus as an infant in Luke 2:8-20 and Matthew 2:1-12.

Discuss these questions with your partner:

- **How did humble shepherds—who were common people—honor Jesus?**

- **What do their actions reveal about their beliefs about Jesus?**

- **How did the Magi—who were prestigious people—honor Jesus?**

- **What do their actions reveal about their beliefs about Jesus?**

These two sets of visitors were very different. The shepherds were working-class folks. They probably smelled a bit like sheep. They weren't rich. They probably weren't educated. The Magi, on the other hand, were likely men of great prestige. They visited with royalty, were likely highly educated, and had significant wealth. Yet both sets of visitors honored Jesus. *Anyone* can kneel before Jesus, recognize him for who he is, and honor him wholeheartedly.

How can you be like the shepherds and honor Jesus with your heart? How can you be like the Magi and honor Jesus with your possessions or material things? Share your thoughts on these two questions with your partner.

Now consider how you can give Jesus a gift of honor—what's one thing you can do this week to honor him? Write down one specific commitment, fold it up, and put it in the gift box.

Then tell your partner what you wrote, and pray for each other as you determine to act on your commitment.

Take a few minutes to write down a few notes from this station on page 14. What stood out to you the most? Why? And be sure to write your answer to this question:

- **What do we learn about Jesus—his traits and his purpose—from these Scripture passages?**

When you're done taking notes, move to the next station with your partner.

Study and Worship Station Notes

STATION A NOTES:

....

....

....

....

....

....

STATION B NOTES:

....

....

....

....

....

....

....

STATION C NOTES:

....

....

....

....

....

....

....

· · · · · · · ·

O Holy Night

by Placide Cappeau

O holy night, the stars are brightly shining;
It is the night of the dear Savior's birth!
Long lay the world in sin and error pining,
Till He appeared and the soul felt its worth.
A thrill of hope, the weary soul rejoices,
For yonder breaks a new and glorious morn.
Fall on your knees, O hear the angel voices!
O night divine, O night when Christ was born!
O night, O holy night, O night divine!

· · · · · · · ·

The Baptism—the Son of God

This is when it all started. Jesus went to the Jordan to be publicly baptized by his cousin John. The sky cracked open; the Holy Spirit could be seen by the naked eye; the voice of the Father identified Jesus as the Son of God. This was the amazing, out-of-this-world launch of Jesus' ministry. Like a catalyst in a chemistry experiment, this baptism triggered a reaction that ended up changing the world.

Up to this point, Jesus had apparently worked with his father Joseph as a carpenter. After his baptism, Jesus began his earthly ministry. People heard the words of John, declaring Jesus to be the Christ. Disciples started to join him. He soon began working miracles, preaching, and teaching…and lives started changing.

> "In his baptism Jesus identified with sinners, something which even John the Baptist found scandalous (Mt. 3:14). It was an anticipation of Calvary, when his cross was to be his baptism—in blood…The baptism of Jesus was an assurance of sonship…[and] it was a commissioning for costly service."
>
> —Michael Green, *The Complete Book of Everyday Christianity*

ON YOUR OWN

Use these ideas as part of your personal devotional time this week.

• •

Read about John the Baptist's death in Mark 6:14-29. How does his death impact your understanding of his life? Why?

• •

Like Andrew, spend an extended amount of time with Jesus getting to know him. Read John chapters 2–5 and reflect on what you learn about Jesus.

• •

Read the quote from Michael Green, and journal about your personal response to it.

NOTES, THOUGHTS, AND PRAYERS...

Research Guide

(Circle one)

John's infancy   John's adult years   Key Scriptures: _____

Instructions: Read your assigned Scripture and discuss it with your group. What do these verses teach you about John the Baptist? Use several Bible study tools to learn more—find additional verses; look up important terms; discover more about John.

NOTES:

....

....

....

....

KEY VERSES IN PASSAGE:

....

....

KEY INSIGHTS FROM STUDY TOOLS:

....

....

CONCLUSIONS:

What were the significant events or circumstances in John's life?

....

....

What were John's characteristics and traits?

....

....

What else stood out to you?

....

....

Prayer and Reflection

Who do you most relate to in this story?

- **John,** who already believed Jesus was the Messiah? If so, how can you be more like John and effectively point others to Jesus? What do you learn from John's example? Write a prayer to God (below) about your desire to point others to Jesus.

- Or **Andrew,** who desired to spend time with Jesus to get to know him better and to come to his own conclusions about Jesus? If so, what questions do you have about Jesus? What do you like about Jesus? How will you try to know Jesus better? Write a prayer (below) about how you'd like to get to know Jesus better.

Dear God...

....

....

....

....

....

....

....

....

....

....

....

....

....

....

Amen

The Disciples—the Cost of Following

Jesus was front-page news in his day. Massive crowds followed him, flocking to hear his revolutionary preaching or to see a fantastic miracle. Often the crowds were so big that Jesus had to get onto a boat to get away and to have a few moments alone. Jesus also often spent time with his closest friends—people like Mary Magdalene, Lazarus, and Lazarus' sisters Mary and Martha. But Jesus' tight-knit group of 12 followers—the disciples—were the ones Jesus would eventually train and entrust to spread his message to the world. The disciples gave up everything to follow Jesus—and most of them eventually gave up their lives for him.

Was it worth it? *Definitely.*

"I know Jesus' followers often enlist with high aspirations and expectations. Disciples step in line with unspoken yet heartfelt agendas…*I know where Jesus will take me,* the young disciples claim, and so they, like the first five [disciples], follow. And they, like the first five, are surprised." —Max Lucado, **When God Whispers Your Name**

Use these ideas as part of your personal devotional time this week.

• •

Read Romans 5:3-5 and 2 Corinthians 11:21b-31. What are Paul's thoughts on suffering? For Paul, was suffering as a follower of Jesus worth it? Is it worth it for you?

• •

Learn more about Christians who are persecuted today. Check out "The Voice of the Martyrs" at www.persecution.com.

• •

Read the quote from Max Lucado, and journal your personal response to it.

NOTES, THOUGHTS, AND PRAYERS...

Light of the World

Jesus called his disciples to him.
These are the names of the apostles:
first, **Simon** *(who is called Peter)*
and his brother **Andrew***;*
James *son of Zebedee,*
and his brother **John***;*
Philip
and **Bartholomew***;*
Thomas
and **Matthew** *the tax collector;*
James *son of Alphaeus,*
and Thaddaeus **(Jude)***;*
Simon *the Zealot*
and **Judas** *Iscariot, who betrayed him.*

How many are there? Count them.

What would it have been like to be one of them? Difficult? Easy?

Step into their shoes. What would it be like to leave everything you have?

You form new friendships. You live a totally different life. Everything is changed.

The center of your life is now the light of the world, Jesus. You and your friends, the others who have chosen the same life as yours, are disciples. What does that mean?

NOTES:

....
....
....
....
....
....
....
....
....
....
....
....
....
....
....

Study 5

The Power—the Miracles of Jesus

Water into wine. Walking on water. Casting out demons. Healing the physically disabled. Giving sight to the blind. Curing the diseased. Calming storms. Feeding massive crowds. Calling the dead back to life. Jesus' power was—and is—unrivaled in the history of humankind. Why? Because he was and is God. The power that created the universe is in his hands. His authority over nature, over disease, and over the devil have been displayed for all to see. The disciples, in shock and amazement, asked, "Who is this? Even the wind and waves obey him!" We too must answer this question. Who *is* Jesus to you? How have you seen his power displayed? How fully do you recognize his authority?

"Although [the disciples] were in a great storm, *the power that made the storm was the very power to which they had to trust.* There was not a single blast of the tempest but Jehovah's might had sent it, nor did a single wave leap up, in apparent wrath, but with God's permission."
—Charles Haddon Spurgeon, ***The CH Spurgeon Collection, Volume 3: Miracles***

ON YOUR OWN

Use these ideas as part of your personal devotional time this week.

••

Study other miracle accounts in Mark 2:1-12; John 2:1-11; and John 9:1-15. What do these miracles teach you about Jesus' personality and character?

••

Go on a nature walk alone or with a friend. Quietly observe small details like tiny insects or intricately designed leaves. Pray as you walk, praising God for Jesus' authority over nature.

••

Read the quote from Charles Spurgeon, and journal about your personal response to it.

NOTES, THOUGHTS, AND PRAYERS...

Inductive Bible Study Guide

SCRIPTURE PASSAGE:

Read the full passage, then identify and name the two miracles in your passage.

Miracle 1: ....

Miracle 2: ....

Discuss these questions for each miracle and write down your answers.

MIRACLE 1

What did Jesus do or say? What is miraculous about it?

....

....

....

How did the people involved in the miracle respond to Jesus?

....

....

....

What did this miracle reveal about who Jesus was? What power or authority did he express?

....

....

....

Key verse or phrase from this miracle passage:

....

....

....

Questions I have about this passage:

....

....

....

MIRACLE 2

What did Jesus do or say? What is miraculous about it?

....

....

....

How did the people involved in the miracle respond to Jesus?

....

....

....

What did this miracle reveal about who Jesus was? What power or authority did he express?

....

....

....

Key verse or phrase from this miracle passage:

....

....

....

Questions I have about this passage:

....

....

....

LIFE APPLICATION

How does the power or authority of Jesus expressed in these miracles make a difference in your life today?

....

....

....

The Recognition—
Jesus' Identity and Mission

It all came down to this moment. The disciples and the crowds had seen his power. There were lots of popular opinions and questions about Jesus' identity. Was he a prophet? Was he a great teacher? The disciples now had to decide what they believed about Jesus.

Jesus asked them squarely who they believed he was—and Peter stepped up to the plate: "You are the Christ!"

Jesus went on to explain the true mission of the Christ: to die and then be raised to life. Just six days later he revealed a glimpse of his true glory to his inner three disciples, Peter, James, and John. They began to see Jesus for who he truly was.

How do you see Jesus? How would you answer his question: "Who do you say that I am?"

> "Today, everyone has an opinion about Jesus, and these opinions range from the traditional to the novel to the heretical...The earnest seeker of truth should move beyond a subjective image of Jesus toward an objective knowledge of who he really is."
> —Douglas Groothuis, *Jesus in an Age of Controversy*

ON YOUR OWN

Use these ideas as part of your personal devotional time this week.

••

Study Matthew 7:21-23. We may call Jesus "Lord" (or Christ), but what does it mean to *know* him? How can you get to know him better?

••

Watch the movie *Whale Rider.* Paikea was a promised leader, but her leadership wasn't recognized until late in the film. Compare and contrast the story of Paikea as the coming chief to Jesus as the prophesied Messiah. How is this story similar to or different from the accounts of Jesus? How does the character Koro (Paikea's grandfather) compare to the disciples who were slow to believe?

••

Read the quote from Douglas Groothuis, and journal your personal response to it.

NOTES, THOUGHTS, AND PRAYERS...

The Christ, the Son of the Living God

The name "Christ" is from the Greek *Christos* and is the New Testament equivalent of the Old Testament Hebrew term that means "Messiah." Its literal meaning is "anointed," or "anointed one," and it refers to someone who was anointed as a leader, such as a priest or a king. Yet when Peter called Jesus "the Christ," he was calling him more than a leader. He was referring to Jesus as the prophesied Messiah, a coming leader of Israel from the line of David who was expected to bring about a "golden age" to Israel and to bring salvation and hope.

When Peter called Jesus "the Son of the living God," he added an extra dimension to his declaration that Jesus was the Christ. Some saw the coming Messiah as only a human leader, but Peter also acknowledged Jesus' identity as God's Son.

Peter's Journal

JOURNAL ENTRY 1

....

....

....

....

....

....

....

....

....

....

....

JOURNAL ENTRY 2

....

....

....

....

....

....

....

....

....

....

....

....

The Stone or the Cross?

Though it's popular and spiritually easy to relegate Jesus to "good guy from history" status, it's simply not an option. *He claimed to be God.* Each and every one of us must decide what we believe about that claim. Was he a crazy man? Was he a blasphemous liar? Or was he telling the truth? And if we believe he was telling the truth, what are the implications of our belief? How should that change how we live? Many of the religious leaders believed Jesus was a dangerous man, blaspheming the holy and true God. Their response was to have Jesus killed. Others, though, accepted Jesus' claim and put their own lives on the line as a consequence. What about you? The stone or the cross?

> "Really, if Jesus of Nazareth was not Christ, He must have been Antichrist." —G.K. Chesterton, **Orthodoxy**

ON YOUR OWN

Use these ideas as part of your personal devotional time this week.

• •

Read Matthew 16:24 in several different versions (translations) of the Bible. One place you can find several versions is on www.biblegateway .com. What are the similarities or differences in language? Which words stand out to you? Journal your thoughts.

• •

Write a poem answering the question: What does it really mean to take up your cross?

• •

Read the quote from G.K. Chesterton, and journal about your personal response to it.

NOTES, THOUGHTS, AND PRAYERS...

_____

_____

_____

_____

_____

_____

_____

_____

_____

_____

_____

_____

_____

Cult Leader Case Studies

MARSHALL HERFF APPLEWHITE

Marshall Applewhite grew up as the son of a Presbyterian minister. He was a good student and was talented in music and drama. As an adult, he married, had children, worked as a music teacher, and directed his church choir. But things changed in 1972 (when he was 41 years old)—he left his family after having a near-death experience. He moved in with a new girlfriend named Bonnie (a nurse from the hospital) and joined a cult group she was a part of. They cut off all ties to their families, changed their names to "Ti" and "Do," and within three years started claiming they were space aliens. Applewhite developed a devoted following, teaching that humans were going to be "re-cycled" by aliens; his group came to be known as the Heaven's Gate cult, and they propagated their beliefs over the Internet. In 1997 the group believed that an alien spaceship was traveling behind the Hale-Bopp comet, which was within view of Earth. Thirty-nine members of the group all gathered in a house in the San Diego area and committed suicide in order to be free from their bodies (which they called "containers") and to allow their spirits to join the aliens in the ship. The cult members killed themselves by helping to feed each other a poisonous drink.

• •

JIM JONES

Jim Jones started out as a Christian pastor in Indianapolis, Indiana. In the '70s he and his church relocated to San Francisco; the church, called the "Peoples Temple," grew to as many as 8,000 churchgoers. The church was very popular because it was racially diverse and addressed important social issues like poverty. But when Jones began receiving criticism, he and about 1,000 church members moved to Guyana (in South America) to develop their own utopian community.

Things began to go awry as Jones exercised greater degrees of control over the group by enforcing strict work hours and using armed guards to keep everyone inside the compound. He began showing signs of extreme paranoia and claimed to be both Jesus and Lenin reincarnate. Food grew scarce and members of the group suffered from malnutrition and illness.

One group member, Deborah Layton, escaped into the jungle and went to get help. A U.S. representative and several reporters responded and went to the compound, only to be attacked and murdered by group members. Soon after, Jones led the group in a mass suicide, forcing them to drink poisoned punch. Those who wouldn't drink it were shot. Some group members escaped into the jungle, but 913 members (including Jones) were later found dead at the scene.

• •

SHOKO ASAHARA

Shoko Asahara was raised in a poor family in Japan. As a young man he started teaching yoga classes in Tokyo; from these classes he developed a cult called *Aum Shinrikyo,* which means "Supreme Truth." Asahara taught that followers could levitate, read minds, and develop other spiritual powers. At its height of popularity, Aum Shinrikyo had over 40,000 members. Cult members began living in compounds where they secretly developed biochemical weapons and followed Asahara's orders, including taking drugs and starving themselves. Asahara's group killed their enemies in human-sized microwave ovens and believed Asahara's claims to be Jesus Christ, Buddha, and Shiva (a Hindu god).

In 1995, in response to a police investigation into their group, Aum Shinrikyo members released sarin gas (a deadly poison) on a Tokyo subway, killing and seriously injuring thousands of passengers. Asahara has been arrested and is in a long and arduous trial process in Japan that could last 15 years. He is charged with murder and faces the death penalty.

Aum Shinrikyo cult compounds still exist in Japan.

DAVID KORESH

Vernon Howell, who later changed his name to David Koresh, was raised by his single mom, who was a young teenager when he was born. Though he was a bad student with few friends, he was very interested in the Bible and as a teenager had memorized large portions of Scripture. He was involved in church as a young man, but was soon kicked out because of his bad influence on others. After an unsuccessful attempt to become a rock star, he joined the Branch Davidians cult in Waco, Texas.

Koresh rose to power in the Branch Davidian cult. He sometimes claimed to be Jesus Christ, saying he had opened the seven seals spoken of in the book of Revelation and speaking of God as his father. He had several wives in the cult—some of whom were as young as 12 or 13 years old—and over a dozen children. He severely disciplined the children, including withholding food for a full day as a punishment, and he regularly taught about an upcoming holy war.

In 1993, the Branch Davidian compound was stormed by the U.S. federal government in their search for illegally stockpiled weapons. The Branch Davidians set off explosives, and over 70 of their members died in the blaze.

NOTES

GROUP NUMBER:......................................

Context:

....
....
....
....
....
....

Historical Background:

....
....
....
....
....
....
....

Why did they want to kill Jesus?

....
....
....
....
....
....
....

Why wasn't Jesus killed?

....

....

....

....

....

....

....

....

What does this story tell us about who Jesus was?

....

....

....

....

....

....

....

....

....

....

....

....

....

....

....

....

....

Following Jesus

Matthew 16:24 says, "Then Jesus said to his disciples, 'If anyone would come after me, he must deny himself and take up his cross and follow me.'" What did Jesus mean? Look at each phrase below, then explain each phrase in your own words, writing one sentence for each phrase.

"DENY HIMSELF"

....

....

....

....

....

....

....

....

"TAKE UP HIS CROSS"

....

....

....

....

....

....

....

....

"FOLLOW ME"

....
....
....
....
....
....
....
....

The Values of Jesus' Kingdom—Service

Think of society's superstars: actors, musicians, athletes, politicians. In worldly terms, these people are the greatest. But what does it take to be the greatest in Jesus' kingdom? Servanthood.

In this me-first world, living out the kingdom value of service definitely goes against the grain. Serving enemies, showing humility, and putting others' needs ahead of your own aren't actions that will put you on the front page of a celebrity magazine, yet these qualities are the identifying marks of true citizens of Jesus' kingdom.

Want to be the greatest? Become a servant.

> "[T]he kingdom of God points to an inverted, upside-down way of life that challenges the prevailing social order…Kingdom values challenge the taken-for-granted social ruts and sometimes run against the dominant cultural grain…Kingdom values, rooted in the deep Love and abiding Grace of God, seed new ways of thinking and living"
> —Donald B. Kraybill, *The Upside-Down Kingdom*

Use these ideas as part of your personal devotional time this week.

••

Study Matthew 6:2-4; Luke 12:32-34; and 1 Timothy 6:18. What do these passages say about generosity? Is your life characterized by this type of generosity? How is generosity related to a heart of servanthood?

••

President John F. Kennedy said, "Ask not what your country can do for you; ask what you can do for your country." Though this quote is about civic life, how could it relate to spiritual life if you changed the words to "Ask not what your God can do for you..." or "Ask not what your church can do for you..."? How could this mind-set shift help you live out Jesus' teachings? Journal your thoughts.

••

Read the quote from Donald Kraybill, and journal about your personal response to it.

NOTES, THOUGHTS, AND PRAYERS...

Kingdom Values

STATION A

Discuss these questions with your partner:

- It is often said that "time is money", and also that "money is power." What do people mean when they say these things?
- What is the role of money in our society? Where does it land in the cultural value system—is it highly valued, mildly valued, or not valued much? Explain.
- Where is money in your personal value system—is it highly valued, mildly valued, or not valued much? Explain.

Now pick up a penny and hold it tightly in your hand, squeezing it hard. As you do, consider how tightly you hold on to your own money, possessions, or time. Keep squeezing while you read the story in Matthew 19:16-22.

Why couldn't the young man do what Jesus asked? If you were the man, how would you feel? Why is it hard to give up money, possessions, or time to serve others? Discuss this story—and the challenge of generosity—with your partner. Also talk about the Kingdom Value regarding money that Jesus reveals in verse 21.

Now open your hand and toss the penny into the "wishing well" (the bowl of water). As you do, say a silent prayer asking God to help you be open-handed and generous as you consider the needs of others.

STATION B

Close your eyes for a moment and picture the person you know who is the hardest to serve or hardest to love. Once you've decided on someone, tell your partner why you picked that person (but don't reveal the person's identity).

Now read Matthew 5:38-48 together. Use the scissors to cut out a human figure from the "Hard to Serve" handouts.

Some people practice voodoo—a false religion. An aspect of voodoo that many people know about is "voodoo dolls"—human figures that people will stick pins in or curse in an effort to get vengeance or wish bad luck upon an enemy. Yet Jesus taught that Christians are to bless their enemies instead of cursing them. Consider your "enemy"—the person you pictured earlier. What is one need your enemy has (whether he or she admits it or not)? Does he or she need encouragement, need friends, need support, or need prayer? Instead of a curse, write on the figure you cut out a word that represents the need you've identified.

Tell your partner one way you can "go the extra mile" for that enemy and serve the person by trying to meet that need. Then tape the figure to the wall.

STATION C

Read John 13:1-17 together, then discuss:

- **What was Jesus trying to teach his disciples concerning service by washing their feet?**
- **Why do you think Jesus used action to teach this lesson instead of just words emphasizing the importance of serving others?**
- **What did Jesus mean in verse 15? How can we follow his example?**
- **When it comes to helping others, what's the difference between good intentions and action?**
- **Why do we often stop short of actually taking action on our good intentions?**

Tell your partner about a recent time you were a servant—what was it like? Why did you do it?

Now go to the poster and add three specific ideas to the service projects brainstorm list. That's right—three ideas *per person*. Think of three practical ways you could do something big or small to serve someone in need.

Now review the list on the poster and read all of the other ideas on it. Select one idea that you're going to put into action this week, then write it here: ....

....

....

The Values of Jesus' Kingdom—Love

Jesus was called a lot of names by those who didn't like him. But one of those names stands out as a badge of honor: They called him a "friend of sinners" (Matthew 11:19). Pious religious folks were shocked that Jesus would show kindness to tax collectors (those dirty rats!), would befriend prostitutes and people who were sleeping around (oh, my!), and would talk to and even touch lepers (aren't they contagious?!?!?).

It's a good thing Jesus bore the title "friend of sinners," because that word *sinners* includes us.

Jesus' kingdom is for everybody—the good, the bad, and the ugly—who chooses to receive his love and respond to his call of discipleship. As citizens of his kingdom, we're called to exhibit his radical, life-changing love.

> "Christian love grants the beloved all his imperfections and weaknesses and in all his changes remains with him, loving the person it sees. If this were not so, Christ would never have loved, for where could he have found the perfect man!" —Søren Kierkegaard, ***Works of Love***

ON YOUR OWN

Use these ideas as part of your personal devotional time this week.

•••

Study Luke 18:9-14. What areas of sinfulness do you need to recognize in your own life? How do you need to better express gratitude for Jesus' love and mercy toward you? Journal your thoughts.

•••

Watch the movie *Les Misérables* (1998) and consider what it teaches about love and grace. If you're a bookworm, consider reading an abridged version of the novel by Victor Hugo. How does the priest's love and grace change Jean Valjean? How is Jean Valjean an example of Jesus' type of love? Are you more like Javert or Valjean? Think about why that is.

•••

Read the quote from Søren Kierkegaard, and journal your personal response to it.

NOTES, THOUGHTS, AND PRAYERS...

Jesus' Radical Love

ASSIGNED SCRIPTURE PASSAGE(S): ....

Read your assigned verses, then discuss these questions with your group and take notes.

What did you learn about Jesus? What is his love like?

....
....
....
....
....
....

How does Jesus' love affect others in the story (or stories)?

....
....
....
....
....
....

What is a key verse or phrase in the passage that characterizes Jesus' love? Write it here:

....
....
....
....
....
....
....

What kind of person today might be considered to be like the outcast(s) in your Scripture passage(s)?

....
....
....
....
....

How does society normally treat them? How does the church treat them?

....
....
....
....
....

How might Jesus treat those people if he walked on earth right now? Describe an imaginary scenario.

....
....
....
....

How should we show Jesus' love and follow his example in the way we treat them?

....
....
....
....
....

Jesus' Love Object Lesson

Look at the object you selected and consider these questions:

What is the purpose of the object?

What does it do? How does it function?

What makes it unique?

How could this object symbolize Jesus' love? How might it relate to the Bible story (or stories) you studied?

Think creatively, then decide how you'll finish this sentence:

Jesus' love is like_____(the object)_____; it...

For example, you might say: "Jesus' love is like a stapler; it mends the hurts, rips, and tears in people's lives. It helps put people back together."

Or "Jesus' love is like a tennis shoe; it helps people walk tall! It helps people take steps in their relationship with God. It fits anyone's feet!"

IDEAS:

....

....

....

....

....

....

....

....

....

....

....

....

....

....

....

O For a Thousand Tongues to Sing

by Charles Wesley (stanzas 7, 14, 15, and 16)

O for a thousand tongues to sing
my great Redeemer's praise!
The glories of my God and King,
the triumphs of his grace.

See all your sins on Jesus laid;
the Lamb of God was slain,
his soul was once an offering made
for every soul of man.

Harlots and publicans and thieves,
in holy triumph join!
Saved is the sinner that believes
from crimes as great as mine.

Murderers and all ye hellish crew,
ye sons of lust and pride,
believe the Savior died for you;
for me the Savior died.

The Crucifixion—Jesus as the Lamb

From the very moment of his baptism—when he was first recognized as the Lamb of God—we see that Jesus has fixed his eyes on the cross. Throughout his ministry of preaching, teaching, and healing, Jesus is determined and undaunted in his passionate pursuit of the cross. He knows his ultimate mission and will not be deterred.

One of the most powerful scenes in Mel Gibson's movie *The Passion of the Christ* is right before Jesus is nailed to the cross. He's fallen to the ground, but instead of waiting for the guards to lay him on the cross, he gets on his hands and knees and crawls to the cross, laying himself down on it to be crucified. This scene visually captures the essence of what Jesus meant when he said, "I lay down my life…No one takes it from me, but I lay it down of my own accord" (John 10:17-18).

Jesus' death was not just a bloody execution—it was filled with divine meaning. It was the moment when the penalty for our sins was paid. Jesus was the sacrifice for our atonement, dying so that we can experience a true relationship—an "at-one-ment"—with the loving, majestic creator God. As Isaac Watts wrote so poignantly, "Love so amazing, so divine, demands my soul, my life, my all."

"There, where the cross stands, the resurrection is near; even there, where everyone begins to doubt God, where everyone despairs of God's power, there God is whole, there Christ is active and near…Where the power of darkness does violence to the light of God, there God triumphs and judges the darkness." —Dietrich Bonhoeffer, from a sermon in *A Testament to Freedom*

ON YOUR OWN

Use these ideas as part of your personal devotional time this week.

••

Study Mark 14:32–15:47. How do you feel as you read about these events? Why? What words or phrases stand out to you most? Why?

••

Review the hymn "When I Survey the Wondrous Cross," then rewrite each line in your own words, reflecting your thoughts and feelings when you think about Jesus' death on the cross.

••

Read the quote from Dietrich Bonhoeffer, and journal your personal response to it.

NOTES, THOUGHTS, AND PRAYERS...

Storyboard Groups

Circle your group's assignment:

The Passover Lamb
Exodus 12:1-11, 21-23

The Sacrificial Lamb
Leviticus 4:32-35 and Numbers 28:1-8

Read your group's verses, then discuss these questions:

• What's the context? Who, what, where, when, why?

• What was the purpose of the lamb?

• Why was it killed?

• Why was this practice of killing the lamb repeated throughout history?

NOTES:

....

....

....

....

....

....

....

....

....

....

....

....

....

....

Your group's job is to create storyboards that explain the key elements of the Scripture passage(s) you studied. A storyboard is something that movie producers or TV show writers use to map out the plot of an episode or film. Each poster depicts a scene or an event. You can use humorous illustrations (like a comic strip), or you can take a more serious tone. For example, here's what a storyboard depicting the meaning of the word *Christ* might look like:

You'll use your storyboards to explain the concept and Scripture passage(s) you studied to the other group, so work together to determine:

- What you want to emphasize in your storyboard (sequence, name or theme of each poster, and so on)

- How you can creatively depict it (for example, using characters and making up a mini-plot)

- How many "scenes" or posters you'll need and what will be depicted on each one

- Who will do what

Make sure every team member is working on a poster, and use crayons and markers to draw pictures, write important words, or define critical concepts.

When you're done, decide who will present your storyboards to the other team.

Definitions of Terms

- *Righteousness of God:* God's faithfulness to carry out his plan of salvation for us through Jesus.
- *Justified:* Acquitted of guilt; declared innocent from the charge of sin.
- *Redemption:* Set free through the payment of a debt; ransomed.
- *Sacrifice of atonement:* The removal of sin and the turning away of God's wrath through the sacrifice of Jesus.

NOTES:

· · · · · · · ·

When I Survey the Wondrous Cross
by Isaac Watts

When I survey the wondrous cross on which
the Prince of glory died,
My richest gain I count but loss, and pour
contempt on all my pride.

Forbid it, Lord, that I should boast save in
the death of Christ, my God.
All the vain things that charm me most,
I sacrifice them to his blood.

See, from his head, his hands, his feet,
sorrow and love flow mingled down.
Did e'er such love and sorrow meet or
thorns compose so rich a crown?

Were the whole realm of nature mine, that
were an offering far too small;
Love so amazing, so divine, demands my
soul, my life, my all.

· · · · · · · ·

The Resurrection—Jesus Conquers Death

Without Easter Sunday, Christianity would look similar to most other religions. It would include inspiring stories and guidance for how to live, and it would tell about a religious leader...who died. And that would be the end of it.

But Jesus didn't stay dead. He rose to life, proving that he was God, demonstrating that he'd paid the penalty for our sins, conquering death, and opening the way for us to live eternally with him in heaven. The truth of Jesus' resurrection is at the core of Christian belief—for his new life is a symbol of death's defeat, Jesus' victory, and *our new* lives! As Paul wrote in Romans 6:4, "We were therefore buried with him through baptism into death in order that, just as Christ was raised from the dead through the glory of the Father, we too may live a new life."

Christianity stands apart, atop all the other religions of the world. Christianity is unique because it is about more than an important and dead historical figure—Jesus is a risen Savior. He is alive. He is risen indeed!

"Easter gives the next piece of the story begun at Christmas and continued into Good Friday. He lived for us and then He died for us and then He rose for us. His death atoned for our sins and His resurrection opens the door to everlasting life." —Lauren F. Winner, **Girl Meets God**

Use these ideas as part of your personal devotional time this week.

••

Study Mark 14:32–15:47. How do you feel as you read about these
Study these verses: John 11:25-26; Romans 6:3-5; and 1 Peter 1:3-4. How
do they shed new light on your understanding of Jesus' resurrection?

••

Select one of the quotes or creeds from "Christian Confessions" (pp. 59-
60) to incorporate into your prayer life. Say the quote each morning
before you start your day.

••

Read the quote from Lauren Winner, and journal your personal response
to it.

NOTES, THOUGHTS, AND PRAYERS...

To Believe or Not to Believe— That Is the Question

Take a moment to silently read through these questions and write your own answers. When everyone in your small group is done, discuss your answers with each other and write down any other insights or notes.

What reasons might someone have to *not* believe in Jesus' resurrection?

....

....

What are the implications of that belief? In other words, how does that affect a person's view of...

death?

....

....

faith?

....

....

who Jesus was?

....

....

If Jesus hadn't risen from the dead, would there be a point to Christianity? If so, what? If not, why not?

....

....

Can a person be a Christian if he or she doesn't believe Jesus rose from the dead? Explain.

....

....

1. "For what I received I passed on to you as of first importance: that Christ died for our sins according to the Scriptures, that he was buried, that he was raised on the third day according to the Scriptures, and that he appeared to Peter, and then to the Twelve. After that, he appeared to more than five hundred of the brothers at the same time, most of whom are still living, though some have fallen asleep. Then he appeared to James, then to all the apostles." —the Apostle Paul in 1 Corinthians 15:3-7 (approximately A.D. 55)

2. "The third day [Jesus] arose again from the dead. He ascended into heaven and sits at the right hand of God the Father Almighty, whence He shall come to judge the living and the dead...[I believe in] the resurrection of the body, and life everlasting. Amen." —the Apostles' Creed (late second century)

3. "[The Church believes] in one Jesus Christ, the Son of God, who became incarnate for our salvation...and the resurrection from the dead, and the ascension into heaven in the flesh of the beloved Christ Jesus, our Lord."
—Irenaeus (A.D. 190)

4. "[We believe] that this [Son] was sent by the Father into the virgin and was born of her both man and God, Son of man and Son of God, and was named Jesus Christ: that he suffered, died, and was buried, according to the scriptures, and, having been raised up by the Father and taken back into heaven, sits at the right hand of the Father."
—Tertullian (A.D. 200)

5. "We believe in...one Lord Jesus Christ, the Son of God, begotten of the Father as only begotten...He suffered and the third day he rose, and ascended into the heavens." —the Nicene Creed (A.D. 325)

6. "[Christ] rose from the dead on the third day, ascended into heaven, and sits on the right hand of God, that he may eternally rule and have dominion over all creatures." —the Augsburg Confession (A.D. 1530)

7. "[Jesus] endured most grievous torments immediately in his soul, and most painful suffering in his body; was crucified, and died; was buried, and remained under the power of death, yet saw no corruption. On the third day he arose from the dead, with the same body in which he suffered." —the Westminster Confession of Faith (A.D. 1646)

Implications of the Resurrection

How does Jesus' resurrection impact your view of death? of faith? of Jesus himself? How does your view of the Resurrection affect the way you live? Journal your thoughts below by finishing this sentence:

Jesus Christ, the Son of God, was bodily raised from the dead. This means...

NOTES:

....

....

....

....

....

....

....

....

....

....

....

....

....

....

....

....

....

....

....

....

....

....

....

The Reign of Christ

There's a lot of speculation about the last days—about the Antichrist, about disasters, about what's symbolic and what's literal, about what will happen when. The truth is that there are many different interpretations of Scripture pertaining to the last days, and no one can be 100 percent sure how it will all happen. In fact, Jesus himself warned that even *he* didn't know exactly when he'd return to earth—only the Father knows (Mark 13:32).

But there is one fact we can be absolutely, totally, completely, and utterly sure of: *Jesus will come back.* He will judge the world and fulfill our ultimate hope: He'll defeat sin, pain, and death, and his followers will find everlasting joy and eternal life with God.

In this broken and hurting world, when nothing seems to go right and when we can't find true satisfaction for our weary souls, we long for Jesus. We long to know him and to see him. We long for him to heal and restore all that's messed up in the world. In Revelation, Jesus promised John—and us—"Yes, I am coming soon." John replied—and we wholeheartedly agree—"Amen. Come, Lord Jesus" (Revelation 22:20).

> "If there's anyone who can appear before Aslan without their knees knocking, they're either braver than most or else just silly."
>
> "Then he isn't safe?" said Lucy.
>
> "Safe?" said Mr. Beaver…"Who said anything about safe? 'Course he isn't safe. But he's good. He's the King, I tell you."
>
> —C.S. Lewis, **The Lion, the Witch and the Wardrobe**

Use these ideas as part of your personal devotional time this week.

. . . .

Study Revelation 4:1–5:14. How does this image of heaven impact you? How does the worship of Jesus in this passage affect you?

. . . .

Read the quote from C.S. Lewis' *The Lion, the Witch and the Wardrobe*, and journal your personal response to it. How does the lion Aslan provide an analogy to Jesus?

. . . .

Review your notes from all of the studies in this series. What did you learn about Jesus that truly impacted your life? How has your friendship with Jesus grown stronger? How would you like it to grow? How has your life changed through your encounters with the Christ? Write a prayer to Jesus about your desire to know him more.

NOTES, THOUGHTS, AND PRAYERS...

....

"Worthy is the Lamb, who was slain, to receive power and wealth and wisdom and strength and honor and glory and praise!"
—(Revelation 5:12)

....